T0153454

STAYIN' ALIVE

Published in 2023 by OH!
An Imprint of Welbeck Non-Fiction Limited,
part of Welbeck Publishing Group.
Based in London and Sydney.
www.welbeckpublishing.com

Compilation text © Welbeck Non-Fiction Limited 2022
Design © Welbeck Non-Fiction Limited 2022

ISBN 978-1-80069-360-9

Compiled and written by: Malcolm Croft
Editorial: Victoria Denne
Project manager: Russell Porter
Design: Tony Seddon
Production: Jess Brisley

A CIP catalogue record for this book is available from the British Library

Printed in China

10 9 8 7 6 5 4 3 2 1

STAYIN' ALIVE

THE LITTLE GUIDE TO THE

BEEGEES

CONTENTS

INTRODUCTION

No other band in the history of pop music can compare to the Bee Gees. They've been there, done that, and – quite literally – bought (and sold) the T-shirt.

Think about it...

What other band has had three separate, but equally successful, career reinventions? Name another group where the lead singer is three brothers? What other group has been universally loved one decade, and loathed the next? Is there another group that has been anywhere near as successful as performers *as well as* songwriters for scores of other artists?

The Bee Gees – Barry, Robin and Maurice – are in a world of their own. Unparalleled in success, influence and invention, their millions of fans will remember them as they deserve: as the fourth most successful pop act in history, behind only the Beatles, Michael Jackson and Elvis Presley.

Since 1958, when they formed as the Rattlesnakes, they have sold more than 220 million records, and are second only to Lennon and McCartney for the amount of No.1 songs they have written. With each new decade the band endured, and yet they not only (just about) survived; they reinvented themselves into something even bigger than before, from Beatles-obsessives to disco-inventors, to redefining

MOR adult pop as crooners-de-extraordinaire. They've also experienced family tragedy on a scale that no family deserves, from the death of younger brother Andy, to the years that drove them apart with drug and drink addiction, and the untimely deaths of Maurice in 2002 and Robin in 2012.

(If you don't have the melody of 'Tragedy' ringing around your ears now, you're no Bee Gees fan.)

Like the Beatles before them, the Bee Gees are beloved for their cheeky wit, wisdom and wisecracks – they are street-walkin', jive-talkin', wax-lyricin' quote machines, never ones to take the pop music business they propped up for so long too seriously. And they're no fools either, as so evidently witnessed when they infamously walked out on Clive Anderson's talk show.

This tiny tome is a love letter to the Bee Gees, of this multi-era-defining, omni-genre-spanning family band, and a salute to their song-writing and singing genius, the likes of which popular music will never see strut down the street again.

Barry, Maurice, Robin – thank you for the music.

So, now tell us – *how deep is your Bee Gees love*?

CHAPTER
ONE

ALIVE AND KICKING

For five decades, the three Brothers Gibb
have given the world more earworms,
across more genres of music, than
perhaps any other group in history.
Let's dive in and learn the A-B-C of
the B's and the G's…

The first words John Lennon ever said to me were, 'Scotch and Coke, isn't it?' If he would have offered me cyanide I would have drunk it. They had just come from the photo shoot for the *Sgt. Pepper* album cover, so they were still in the full uniforms and glasses and all that stuff. I couldn't believe it was him at first. That was my first scotch and Coke.

Maurice, on getting to know the Beatles, interview with Aidin Vaziri, *San Francisco Chronicle*, January 27, 2002.

We were born at the age of 12 so we could start singing and make money for our parents right away.

Maurice, speaking of his parents, encouragement to form a group, in an interview with Greg Mitchell, *Crawdaddy* magazine, June 1978.

In the early sixties, the Bee Gees released 11 singles in Australia to little success.

The group, sounding suspiciously a lot like the Beatles, were actually No.1 in New Zealand with their song "Spicks and Specks" when they returned to the UK in 1967.

Within months they were hanging out with Paul, John, George and Ringo, and a plethora of other pop stars.

Before we ever became famous were the best times of our lives. There was no competition; it didn't matter who sang what. When we had our first No.1, 'Massachusetts', Robin sang the lead, and I don't think he ever got past that; he never felt that anyone else should sing lead after that. And that was not the nature of the group. We all brought songs in; whoever brings the idea in sings the song.

Barry, on **Robin**, interview with Alexis Petridis, *Irish Times*, December 15, 2020.

"

I would say the Beatles, Otis Redding and the whole Motown scene really are our biggest influences. There aren't so many contemporary people that would influence me, as there are just far too many cover version artists.

"

Robin Gibb, on inspiration, *Top of the Pops*, 2003.

We are brothers first, a
pop group second.

Barry, discussing the group, interview with
Julia Llewellyn, *Daily Express*, March 29, 2001.

66

The only way I can describe
how we work at it is to
become one mind.

99

Maurice, discussing their song-writing process,
from the 2020 HBO documentary, *The Bee Gees:
How Can You Mend a Broken Heart*.

We never get jealous when somebody has a hit with one of our songs. Because when we give a song away, we give a song away. We don't go back thinking, 'Oh no they've had a big hit and we haven't.'

Robin, on hit-writing for other artists, *Muse*, 2001.

We were street kids. Our parents had no control over us. I had a great fear of the law, but I also was very rebellious. Life on the street became more fun, and we wouldn't come home until 11 at night, 12 at night. We'd be on the streets every night.

Barry, on their naughty years, interview with Michael Odell, *Daily Express*, October 23, 1997

Three tits. Two vaginas.

Robin, when asked what "more than a woman" means, interview with David Wild, *Rolling Stone*, May 29, 1997.

In 1967, the group's first minor hit, 'New York Mining Disaster 1941', sounded so similar to the Beatles that the band's label sent it to radio stations as a white label, with no band listed on the sleeve.

The gimmick worked. DJs played it and listeners believed the song was a new Beatles cut.

One of the reasons for the Bee Gees' success, is that we've never used music as a soap box.

Robin, on keeping politics out of the music, interview by Harvey Kubernik, *Melody Maker*, January 21, 1978.

66

It may be 99 million… and five.

99

Maurice, on being told the band had sold 100 million records, *Taratata*, 1993.

I'm the last person to think I'd still be hearing those songs now or that anybody would be interested in them now. It's a long time ago.

Barry, on his songs' survival, interview with Alexis Petridis, *Irish Times*, December 15, 2020.

CHAPTER
TWO

BROTHERS IN HARMONY

Famed for their tight three-part harmonies and magical song-writing connection, Robin, Maurice and Barry composed hundreds of songs together.

But, as deep as their love was for each other, their bond was also broken several times throughout their brilliant careers…

I have a mental picture of us boys around 1955 in the Manchester suburb of Chorlton-cum-Hardy, after we'd moved from the Isle of Man. We three made a pact as we headed down Keppel Road from school that, come hell or high water, we were going to make it as singers in a band. I think that us walking down that road on that day is still one of the main tempos in our music.

Barry, on early visions of stardom, interview with Timothy White, *Billboard*, February 15, 1997.

"
My dad heard us in our bedroom doing the Everly Brothers and he thought the radio must be on.
"

Maurice, on his dad hearing them sing together for the first time, interview by Julia Llewellyn, *Daily Express*, March 29, 2001.

I was Mr. Goody Two Shoes, because on my one and only crime spree, lifting a bottle of orange juice off a doorstep, I was caught and three policemen walked me home. But Barry and Robin were pilfering left, right and centre from Woolies.

Maurice, on his youthful misdemeanours, interview by Johnny Black, *Mojo*, June 2001.

66

I was a bit of a fire bug when
I was about 8 years old,
especially around the streets of
Manchester. For some unknown
reason I used to go around
and light fires on golf courses
and a few dream homes too
perhaps, but that was only if
they got in the way. It was just
after that that we emigrated…

99

Robin, on his love of arson during his youth,
Frank Skinner Live, October 29, 2002.

1978 is remembered as "The Year of the Bee Gees". They were undoubtedly the biggest group in the world.

They released eight singles that all reached No.1 around the world, a feat yet to be beaten, and accounted for 2 per cent of the worldwide record industry sales (roughly $1 out of every $50 spent).

"How Deep Is Your Love"

"Stayin' Alive"

"Night Fever"

"Too Much Heaven"

"(Love Is) Thicker Than Water"

"Shadow Dancing"

"Grease"

"If I Can't Have You"

We're all boss of this band at one time or another. If I get really dogged about something and I don't want to do it and everyone else does, my wife Linda will turn 'round and say, 'Get your pants on and go and bloody do it and shut up moaning.'

Barry, on who's boss of the band, interview by Johnny Black, *Mojo*, June 2001.

We never set out to make ourselves the kings of disco, although plenty of other people tried to jump on the bandwagon after the success of the film. When we went to the premiere at the Chinese Theatre in Los Angeles it was obvious the film and the songs really gelled, but none of us had any idea how huge it would become. It remains the biggest-selling soundtrack ever, and very few artists have created something with the cultural impact that *Saturday Night Fever* had.

Robin, on *Saturday Night Fever*, *Observer Music Monthly*, January 2008.

"
You know what we need?
We need Dolly Parton.
"

Barry, on "Islands in the Stream", interview by
Craig Shelburne, CMT, February 3, 2006.

There's three of us and there's always been three of us, and since school days it was us three against the world.

Barry, on the Bee Gees, interview by Timothy White, *Rolling Stone*, May 17, 1979.

When we were cutting our song 'Nights on Broadway', [producer] Arif Mardin asked me if I had any falsetto. He wanted somebody singing up high or maybe screaming. So I went out in the studio, and I found that not only could I scream in tune, I could sing a whole song in falsetto.

Barry, on discovering his famous falsetto, *TV Guide*, 1979.

When we arrived in the UK in 1967 we were absolute Beatles lookalikes.

Barry, on being like the Beatles, interview with Alexis Petridis, *Irish Times*, December 15, 2020.

The Brothers Gibb, plus sister Lesley, were born on the Isle of Man to English parents, Barbara and Hugh. They lived in Chorlton, Manchester, until 1958 when they emigrated to Queensland, Australia. The debate raged for decades about whether they were an "Australian band" or not.

We're not a nostalgia act. We're still making contemporary music.

Robin, on the band's relevance, *USA Today*, 1997.

"

We've been shat on
by the best.

"

Barry, discussing the band's once-great
unpopularity, in an interview with Greg Mitchell,
Crawdaddy magazine, June 1978.

I love to write for people.
It is not just thinking, 'Oh,
I will write a song today'.
When someone you admire
asks you to write a song,
that is special motivation.

Barry, discussing song-writing for other artists,
BBC, June 26, 2018.

"

You can't put us in a
category. We're part folk,
pop, rock, R&B, everything.
The tags rarely fit. What
is disco? What is rock?
It's all pretty vague
and ambiguous.

"

Barry, on what makes the Bee Gee sound,
USA Today, 1997.

I've had to deal with loss, not just my brothers but my mother and father. But what I've learned from all of it is that things just roll on, and you roll on with them. 🙲

Barry, on family tragedy, interview with Alexis Petridis, *Irish Times*, December 15, 2020.

I've always been between Barry and Robin. But I am always the decider. It's just been our life that I always end up being the man in the middle. So they call me The Engine.

Maurice Gibb, In Conversation, May 21, 2001.

What song-writing's always been to me is basically like a flash. I have a flash of an idea or a flash of a chorus, or a flash of a song before it's actually constructed. That hasn't changed, it's continued right through my life. I'll get up in the middle of the night and put something on a Dictaphone and go back to sleep.

Barry, on song-writing, *Performing Songwriter*, 1998.

First-fame is a very dangerous thing. You read about yourself, believe what people say about you, you believe that you have something very special to say, and God speaks through you and the public need to know, you know. This happens to you when you become famous for the first time, and especially on an international level.

Barry, on finding fame the first time, VH1, 1997.

A lot of people thought we started with *Saturday Night Fever*, so it became our albatross. Before the film, we were called blue-eyed soul, but after the film we were the kings of disco.

Maurice, on *Saturday Night Fever*, interview with Johnny Black, *Mojo*, May 21, 2001.

We're getting on like a storm, aren't we, Clive. In fact I might just leave. And you're the tosser, pal.

Barry, on the now-infamous walk-out on Clive Anderson's talk show, BBC, 1997.

I've worked with a lot of people who are more famous than myself who are terribly insecure. Michael Jackson once asked me, 'Do you think Prince is better than me?' Can you imagine that, after all he has achieved?

Barry, on Michael Jackson, interview by David Wigg, *Daily Mirror*, March 24, 1998.

Robin and Maurice are twins. Robin is half an hour older than Maurice.

You're always dealing with people who want to tell you what kind of songs you should record.

Barry, on the band's demise in 1969, interview by Timothy White, *Billboard*, March 24, 2001.

There's been big ups and big downs and big fights. But the fights are good. I think the closer you are to somebody, the more likely it is that you fight. In fact it's not healthy that you not fight. A good fight clears the air.

Maurice, on fighting with his brothers, interview by Paul Baratta, *Songwriter Magazine*, February 1978.

What broke us up was Robin and Maurice moving out from our suburban home in Hendon. They went crazy with drink, female pop stars and the rest. We turned our backs on one another. We became obnoxious and arrogant. We didn't take phone calls from each other, we got accountants and lawyers to deal with it.

Barry, on their 1969 break-up, interview by Michael Odell, *Daily Express*, October 23, 1997.

When Andy [younger brother] died, I remember saying to Barry and Robin at the funeral, that we have to stay bonded. We have to be together because without each other, we're nothing. And we realized that, not because of Andy's death. We realized it of all the things we've done years before, we've gone … this cannot happen. We cannot lose each other. And that made our bond much stronger. So that was a tragedy that helped.

Maurice, on the passing of brother Andy, In Conversation, May 21, 2001.

I don't ever wish I was somebody else. I know that I am meant to be who I am, and I'm meant to have my own destiny. Wherever that takes me, I'm sensible enough to accept it no matter what it is. My music, certainly, has never embarrassed me.

Barry, on his love for his own music, interviewed on *Live*, December 1997.

66

The Bee Gees are hot. But sooner or later these bubbles burst anyway, and I would like for the Bee Gees to stop before we wane. I don't know if it's easy or accurate to say that in the next two years the Bee Gees will decline or continue at this pace. None of us can say. But all bubbles have a way of bursting or being deflated in the end.

99

Barry, on their second wave of popularity, *Teen Beat*, January 1980.

The style of writing songs doesn't change at all, really. We have a cassette player in the middle of a table, and we sit around with the guitars and keyboards and shoot out ideas. I don't think you can do it any other way, really. Melody first, lyrics second.

Robin, discussing the band's song-writing sessions, Still Waters Press Kit, 1997.

CHAPTER
THREE

DISCO
BEATLES

The Bee Gees have been called
many things in their long career – the
masters of reinvention, the comeback
kings, Les Tosseurs – but "the Disco
Beatles" is perhaps the best way
to sum up the significance of the group,
in terms of influence, invention
and inspiration.

There's no room for being just a part of yesterday. We want to be part of now. We want to have some relation to music as it is today. We never want people to say, 'Ah, they were the late sixties', or 'They were the late seventies.' People are so decade-oriented. As soon as the decade is over, it's time for all the new artists to come in. We want to override all that.

Robin, on the shelf-life of music, interview by Paul Baratta, *Songwriter Magazine*, February 1978.

"

It's a horrible thing if you've got a 'For Whom the Bell Tolls' and a U.S. radio station says, 'No, we don't want to hear it. It's the Bee Gees, so we're not going to play it.'

"

Barry, on the death of disco and the ridicule of the Bee Gees following its demise, interview by Timothy White, *Billboard*, March 24, 2001.

66

We knew when we came back together that it would take us five or six years to become anything like what we were before we started on the drugs, and before we got fame and huge egos. We had to get to know each other again.

99

Barry, on the 1969 break-up and reconciliation, interview by Timothy White, *Rolling Stone*, May 17, 1979.

Fucking quick. A heart attack onstage would be ideal, right in the middle of 'Stayin' Alive!'

Barry, on how he wants to die, interview with Ella Alexander, *Independent*, July 11, 2014.

Our father never once told us that we were good. Every time we came off stage, he told us we were terrible and I think this is what stopped us from being big-headed.

Robin, on his dad, Hugh, interview with Michael Odell, *Daily Express*, October 23, 1997.

"

We're the enigma with
the stigma.

"

Barry, about the band's reputation, upon being
inducted into the Rock 'n' Roll Hall of Fame, 1997.

You could spin the dial at any time and hear a song from *Saturday Night Fever* on every radio station at any given moment. With exposure like that, there had to be an inevitable backlash.

Robin, on *Saturday Night Fever*, VH1, 1999.

Playing Wembley Stadium had been a dream of ours for years. But what I remember most about it was that we were all up in this room above the stadium watching the crowds stream in and Barry nudged me and said, 'Well, we got away with it. We fooled them again.' And we just laughed ourselves silly, because that's how it's always felt to us – like we're getting away with it and one day somebody will notice.

Maurice, on performing at Wembley Stadium, London, interview with Johnny Black, *Mojo*, May 21, 2001.

The Bee Gees first broke the U.S. charts in 1971 with the song, 'How Can You Mend a Broken Heart?', having broken up two years earlier. They went on to have nine U.S. No.1's.

My greatest accomplishment? Having the most successful catalogue of songs in the world, alongside Lennon and McCartney.

Robin, on his greatest achievement, interview with Rosanna Greenstreet, *Guardian*, July 31, 2010.

Contrary to popular belief, we have no leader. We call it a democratic dictatorship.

Maurice, on who's the band leader, interview with Julia Llewellyn, *Daily Express*, March 29, 2001.

> ❝
> We're just a pop group,
> we're not a political force.
> We're just making music,
> and I don't think there's
> any reason to chalk us
> off because we existed
> in the '70s and we would
> like to exist in the '80s.
> ❞

Barry, discussing the band's unpopularity in the early
1970s, from the 2020 HBO documentary, *The Bee Gees:
How Can You Mend a Broken Heart*.

In the Sixties, everyone was doing drugs, and so did we, but we had limits. We never did LSD or heroin. We loved grass because it helped us create. But we were virginal compared to some others. I remember sitting in a room talking to John Lennon and I didn't realize he was tripping on acid. I just thought he had a very vivid imagination.

Maurice, on John Lennon, Interview with Michael Odell, *Daily Express*, October 23, 1997.

At school we sang to the other kids. They didn't like us much, but we used to stand against the wall, tell jokes and sing. In fact, most choirs we were in at school, we were thrown out of. Most of the schools didn't like us harmonizing to 'God Save The Queen'. We didn't mean to. It's just that we sang it that way, and naturally they said, 'What are you doing? Get out of my class!'

Maurice, on their early musical years, interview with Michael Odell, *Daily Express*, October 23, 1997.

Robin and I were the people who really fought, and Maurice was always on the outside getting the flak. We two were at loggerheads with each other cause he was a songwriter and I'm a songwriter, and his voice and my voice are different. We're two different people but we're both creative, and at that period it was too much for us: who was getting credit on the songs, who was getting voice credit, who should be singing what song. But our problems then were very destructive. Nowadays we don't care.

Barry, on the reasons of the 1969 break-up, interview by Timothy White, *Rolling Stone*, May 17, 1979.

We never made any effort to get into the disco market. We wrote those songs on the *Saturday Night Fever* soundtrack for our new album in France and Robert Stigwood [then manager] called us and asked us if we had any new songs for this film. We knew nothing about disco music. Disco to us was what a club was always called in England and we never knew there was such music as disco, that was a phrase that came up in America after the film came out. We never saw the film till it came out so that music to us was just R&B music we were making for our album.

Robin, on *Saturday Night Fever*, Radio 2, 2001.

I'd like to clear this point up. I know there are rumours that Barry does more on our records than Robin and me. I don't know how that rot got started, but I hate and resent it. It's a load of shit. As far as our records are concerned, we all contribute equally and all produce equally.

Robin, on Barry as band leader, interview by Timothy White, *Rolling Stone*, May 17, 1979.

Robert Stigwood brought their first demo to me and said, 'I've got these Australian lads, what do you think?' And it was the 'Mining Disaster' song that he played me. I said, 'Sign them, they're great!' and they went on to be even greater.

Paul McCartney, on the Bee Gees, interview by Timothy White, *Billboard*, March 24, 2001.

When Barry was 18 months old, he scolded himself so badly with hot tea that doctors told his mother he had 20 minutes to live. "The incredible thing for me is that whole two years is wiped from my memory, the whole period of being in hospital. The idea of being burnt is in there somewhere, but I have no knowledge of it. I've got the scars but I have no knowledge," Barry said later of the accident.

When people say, 'Your brothers are looking down on you and smiling', I don't know if that's true. But maybe, if there's any truth to that stuff, one day I'll bump into my brothers again. And they'll say, 'What kept you?'

Barry, on meeting **Maurice** and **Robin** again, interview with Ella Alexander, *Independent*, July 11, 2014.

We're just three little persistent bastards who want to be as big as the Beatles. That's been our motto since we started.

Maurice, on the group's ambitions, interview with Aidin Vaziri, *San Francisco Chronicle*, January 27, 2002.

In those days everybody used to just hang out. I used to be married to Lulu. So at 2am we'd hear the door knock and it would be David Bowie and Dudley Moore and all these other wonderful people. We'd go down in our dressing gowns and get the bar open, put some music on and have a good time. Or we would go over to the studio where Ringo Starr was hanging out and we'd all jam. And then Jimmy Page and Robert Plant would drop by. Everybody mixed.

Maurice, on early fame, interview with Aidin Vaziri, *San Francisco Chronicle*, January 27, 2002.

We pulled some people out. Molly [Maurice's wife] was bruised and battered. I had glass in my mouth, in my eyes, in my hair, for weeks. It made me realize you could be dead at any minute and you should seize every moment. It wasn't a spiritual experience. I was just very lucky.

Maurice, on his near-death Hither Green train crash*, interview by Johnny Black, *Mojo*, June 2001.

Fifty passengers were killed.

We'd been making our own guitars out of cheese boxes and fuse wire, so Dad bought Barry a cheap guitar. This soldier Dad knew taught Barry how to tune his guitar to an open D, which is still how he plays today.

Maurice, on early music-making, interview by Johnny Black, *Mojo*, June 2001.

It's nice being very popular
by yourself. But it's great
when you can share it.

Robin, on fame with his brothers, *TV Guide*,
November 10, 1979.

> **"**
> Experiment and failure,
> experiment and failure, and
> experiment and success.
> **"**

Barry, on the Bee Gees' guide to success, interview by Paul Baratta, *Songwriter Magazine*, February 1978.

The title is just as important as the song. Once you have the title the rest just flows from there.

Robin, on the importance of song titles, interview by Harvey Kubernik, *Melody Maker*, January 21, 1978.

> **"**
>
> Our dad, who'd been a professional drummer and bandleader for 20 years, was struggling to make ends meet; our mom was ill, and there were five kids. Singing wasn't a question of having a career at that point. It was a question of survival. We started performing between the races at the Redcliffe Speedway in Brisbane, and then we put an act together for the Australian nightclub circuit. That's when we began to have career ambitions.
>
> **"**

Robin, on life in Australia, *TV Guide*, 1979.

The brothers hilariously nicknamed the band "Pot, Pills and Piss" after their substance addictions. Barry was "Pot", Robin was "Pills" and Maurice was "Piss" (booze).

"Barry would be smoking pot, Robin was on pills and I would be drinking," Maurice said.

We had been down on our luck and someone said, 'Would you write some songs about a painter who goes out dancing in the evenings?' so we did. If we'd have known Travolta would make such a good job out of it we wouldn't have knocked out any old rubbish and sung in those stupid voices.

Robin, on *Saturday Night Fever*, interview with Michael Odell, *Daily Express*, October 23, 1997.

'Fever' was No. 1 every week ...
It wasn't just like a hit album. It
was No. 1 every single week for 25
weeks. It was just an amazing, crazy,
extraordinary time. I remember not
being able to answer the phone,
and I remember people climbing
over my walls. I was quite grateful
when it stopped. It was too unreal.
In the long run, your life is better
if it's not like that on a constant
basis. Nice though it was.

Barry, discussing the phenomenon of *Saturday Night Fever*, interview with Sam Kashner, 2007.

Disco was a departure from the ballad style we were most often associated with. When 'Jive Talkin" became a hit, people started saying that we had stepped down to be a disco group which was sort of a put down to disco music as well.

Barry, on disco, interview by Paul Baratta, *Songwriter Magazine*, February 1978.

"
People expect you to
have a naked woman
in every room.

"

Robin, on the perks of fame, interview by
Jim Jerome, *People Magazine*, August 6, 1979.

The minute you sit down and think, 'Oh great, I'm successful!' That leaves you nowhere to go mentally and you go stale. And when you go stale, that's the end of the line, cobber.

Barry, on evolving the sound of the band, interview by Paul Baratta, *Songwriter Magazine*, February 1978.

"

At the speedway, there was a race driver called Bill Goode who knew a disc jockey named Bill Gates. His initials were B.G. ... the Brothers Gibb, B.G., ... my initials are B.G., and Bill Gates suggested that that's what we should call ourselves: the Bee Gees. So, Bill Gates, and Bill Goode the racing driver, got together and came to our house, and said, 'Hey, boys, we want to manage you. We want to promote you.' Bill was the lead disc jockey on a radio station in Brisbane and he made tapes of us and played them on the air. That's how we first got radio play in Australia.

Barry, on the birth of the Bee Gees, interview by Paul Baratta, *Songwriter Magazine*, February 1978.

CHAPTER
FOUR

JIVE TALKIN'

The Bee Gees may have been revered for their "Jive Talkin'", but it was their wit that got them into trouble more. "Someone once said the Bee Gees haven't got a sense of humour," said Maurice. "I said, 'You're kidding!' Everybody who knows us knows we always have a good time."

There's a bridge that we have to cross on the way to the studio. And every time we crossed it, the car would make a clickety-clack sound. After a few days of this, we realized that the clickety-clack rhythm was perfect for a song. And it turned into "Jive Talkin'".

Maurice, on the genesis of "Jive Talkin'",
TG Magazine, September 1978.

We weren't cut out to be solo stars. We were cut out to be the Bee Gees. Somebody in his almighty wisdom knew that, whether we did or not.

Barry, on the Bee Gees, interview by Frank Rose, *Rolling Stone*, July 14, 1977.

66

I can't say that we have ever thought of going punk.

99

Robin, on reinventing the band again,
BBC 5 Live interview, 2001.

I think you've got to stay, at some point, true to your art and you've got to sail between the winds of change, and if you get too trend-orientated, you become that trend.

Robin, on sailing on the winds of change, BBC 5 Live interview, 2001.

In the 1960s, it was Robin's vibrato that was considered the lead vocal of the group.

In the 1970s, Barry's falsetto became the signature sound of their disco period.

In the 80s and 90s, the three-part harmonies of the brothers would define their "adult pop" reinvention.

A lot of people would love to have a *Fever* in their career. It blew us away. Then we got crucified for it. And now we get respect for it.

Maurice, on the albatross of *Saturday Night Fever's* success, interview with Aidin Vaziri, *San Francisco Chronicle*, January 27, 2002.

All we were told was that it was about a Brooklyn guy who works at a paint shop across the bridge in New York and goes out every Saturday night and wins a dance competition. After the film, the world wanted to dance. Lawyers and judges and people who never buy albums, normally, were buying *Saturday Night Fever* and taking dance lessons.

Maurice, on *Saturday Night Fever*, *Entertainment Weekly*, 1999.

Michael [Jackson] started to hang out at the house all the time, and I had to get up in the morning; I'm 12 years older than him; I had to take my kids to school. At some point, I said: 'Michael, wherever it is you're going, you've got to go.' So, I politely asked Michael Jackson to leave my house because I couldn't get anything else done.

Barry, on his friendship with Michael Jackson, interview with Alexis Petridis, *Irish Times*, December 15, 2020.

If you try just writing a hit you lose that 'it', that element that puts you in touch with people. For us a song is also subjective, it's down to each person who listens to it what they think, or how they imagine it involves their life. So we try to write our songs in an abstract form. If we were looking for a hit I don't think we would have one. We have to work for some emotional connection that everyone can relate to in some sort of emotional way.

Barry, discussing the phenomenon of *Saturday Night Fever*, interview with Sam Kashner, 2007.

Bob Dylan sings in the same way as me. He uses his heart as an instrument. Even I can't understand completely why this works but it does. It's not possible for any artist to jump outside themselves and see themselves for what they are. Even when you look in a mirror you get a reversed image!

Robin, on his voice, interview with Keith Altham, Rock's Backpages, August 1969.

I do less singing, of course. I only come in on high harmonies. I'm more of the musician, playing the piano, bass, mellotron or organ on records, which saves money on hiring musicians, for one thing. It's the same when it comes to writing. I write the music, because I cannot really write lyrics. But I can write chords like Robin's never heard of. So I provide the music for them to write the lyrics to.

Maurice, on his role within the group, *Idea Special*, 1968.

The disco backlash hurt at the time, but I've gotten philosophical. A segment of the industry wanted to shed the whole disco movement. We were the heads they put on a stick.

Barry, on the death of disco, *USA Today*, 1997.

I thought the Bee Gees condom was going too far.

Robin, on the band's never-ending supply of merchandise, interview with David Wild, *Rolling Stone*, May 29, 1997.

The Bee Gees testicle tickler was a big seller.

Robin, on the band's never-ending supply of merchandise, interview with David Wild, *Rolling Stone*, May 29, 1997.

"

Our songs are like our kids, and you feel funny favouring one to the other. But sometimes one wanders off, or you have to change its diaper.

"

Robin, on choosing a favourite Bee Gees song, interview by Timothy White, *Billboard*, March 24, 2001.

We thought when we were writing 'Stayin' Alive' that we should emulate the human heart. We got Blue Weaver, who was the keyboard player at the time, to lie on the floor and put electrodes on his heart and put it through the control room. Then we got the drummer to play the heartbeat. We were the first people in the world to do a drum loop based on that.

Robin, on the pulse of "Stayin Alive", interview with Daniel Rachel, *The Art of Noise: Conversations with Great Songwriters*, 2014.

We're songwriters, and we're brothers, and we're much stronger together than we are apart.

Maurice, on family unity, interview by Johnny Black, *Mojo*, June 2001.

Most times it's very
flattering, but often I'm still
not comfortable with it.

Barry, on other artists covering their songs,
Billboard, 1998.

The Brothers Gibb, like the Beatles, are famed for their cheeky wit. They also have roles within the band: Maurice is the backbone, shy and quiet. Robin is the funny one. Barry is the dad of the group.

I never thought of them as my little brothers. It just wasn't like that. There was something we all loved doing, and we kept on doing it. There was nothing more fun than singing in three-part harmony.

Barry, on his brothers, interview with Alexis Petridis, *Irish Times*, December 15, 2020.

I'm very much a family person. I just love the feeling a close family gives you and I wouldn't change it for anything. I've never been into parties, premieres or night-clubbing. I much prefer staying at home with the wife and kids, watching TV or reading a book. I'm Mr Boring, not a party-goer at all.

Barry, on his non-partying days, 1998.

I love to live in love today. I don't live in the negative. I don't think negative. I don't pursue anything that is negative. I don't even ask questions that are negative. I just go for what I enjoy. And love to do what I do. And if I am loving it then it's incredible. That you can do something that you love as you work is a blessing.

Maurice, on loving his work, In Conversation, May 21, 2001.

"

I miss them so much. I can still feel them. I smell my brothers' breath. I get that feeling that they are right there. I feel as if they are there guiding me. I get nerves being on stage on my own because it is so new to me. We would all lean on each other. I'd lean on Maurice and Robin and they would lean on me and somehow we'd get through every show.

"

Barry, on the absence of Maurice and Robin, while on stage during his now-iconic Glastonbury 2017 set, interview with Halina Watts, *Daily Mirror*, June 26, 2017.

Between the mid Seventies and beginning of the Eighties, we were nearly torn apart but we all had a strong friendship... I've always said of that period that I didn't enjoy not being able to answer my own phone. I didn't enjoy people climbing over the walls in my back garden and there are moments in life when those things happen, but that level of fame it isn't consistent and everlasting – it has to have a break.

Barry, on the band's ultra-fame, Muse, 2001.

66
Real men sing falsetto.

99

Barry, on his famous falsetto, interview with David Wild, *Rolling Stone*, May 29, 1997.

We believe in keeping the glamour in show business and that's why we wear suits on stage. You've got to look smart. If you walk out on stage and look like one of the audience, the mystique is gone. They pay to be entertained, and you've got to give them a show for their money. You're supposed to be unreal.

Robin, on looking like a star on stage, interview by Harvey Kubernik, *Melody Maker*, January 21, 1978.

"

The first rock'n'roll record I ever heard was Little Darlin' by The Diamonds – that was falsetto. So in a way it's been an integral part of rock'n'roll. It's nice to be a falsetto that's well known.

"

Barry, on his famous falsetto, interviewed by Johnny Black, *Mojo*, February 1998.

You've got to remember, we weren't doing disco. To us, KC & the Sunshine Band and Donna Summer and the Village People made party disco music. KC, to me, is the king of disco. He was doing it long before anybody else.

Maurice, on the origins of disco, interview with Aidin Vaziri, *San Francisco Chronicle*, January 27, 2002.

We've basically been through the whole in-fighting, drugs, the drink, all the scenarios you can imagine. We've done all that and still survived.

Barry, on the band's survival, interviewed by Johnny Black, *Mojo*, February 1998.

People accuse us of being nothing more than a disco band now. But they don't know what they're talking about.

Maurice, on becoming disco, *TG Magazine*, 1978.

Before they were the Bee Gees, the Brothers Gibb were called the Rattlesnakes.

They made their first public debut in December 1957 at the Gaumont Theatre, Manchester.

66

I care that the music lives, and I do everything in my power to enhance that. That's my mission now.

99

Barry, on keeping the band's legacy alive, interview with Alexis Petridis, *Irish Times*, December 15, 2020.

"

We all have our separate friends and families. If we don't call each other for a couple of months it doesn't mean anything. We've always done it. When we see each other again we just pick right back up.

"

Maurice, on the band's less-than-sociable socializing, interview with Julia Llewellyn, *Daily Express*, March 29, 2001.

We put about thirty percent of what we consider to be our art into our records and about seventy percent of it is us writing for the public. You've got to include both.

Barry, on their songwriting, interview by Timothy White, *Rolling Stone*, May 17, 1979.

Robert Stickweed, er, Stigwood, rang us up and said, 'Look, I need some music for this film I'm making with John Revolting and Olivia Neutron Bomb and – oh, no, that was *Grease*, wasn't it?

Barry, joking about *Saturday Night Fever*, interview by Timothy White, *Rolling Stone*, May 17, 1979.

132

Personalities are examined in 'How Deep is Your Love' but female or male aren't even mentioned. It has universal connotations and it clicks with everyone.

Robin, on "How Deep is Your Love", interview by Harvey Kubernik, *Melody Maker*, January 21, 1978.

CHAPTER
FIVE

TRAGEDIES

When the Bee Gees wrote
their famous hit, "Tragedy", it came
from a place of real-life experience,
with the group experiencing more
than their fair share of death,
self-destruction, addiction, and
ill-health.

But what didn't kill them thankfully
only made them stronger...

We split, we fought, we abused our bodies, lost money, watched loved ones destroy themselves, everything. It's only now we cherish what matters.

Maurice, on their road to stardom, interview by Michael Odell, *Daily Express*, October 23, 1997.

I have a huge ego and a huge inferiority complex at the same time.

Barry, on his ego, interview by David Wigg, *Daily Mirror*, March 24, 1998.

"Stayin' Alive" is known, rather famously, for being the ideal song to employ as a regular rhythm, if called upon to do CPR.

The track has 104 beats per minute, the recommended amount of chest compressions required to, aptly, assist an unconscious person to stay alive.

We never even thought about money. When we had it, we just blew it. I had six Rolls-Royces and eight Aston Martins by the time I was 21! I was invincible in those days. It was that age period when you start discovering new things. I learned more by the time I was 19 than by the time I was 40.

Maurice, on early fame and fortune, interview with Aidin Vaziri, *San Francisco Chronicle*, January 27, 2002.

The Bee Gee wives have no time for our egos. They'll say, 'This is that showbiz ego thing – get rid of it, act your age.' So we're like that with each other, as brothers.

Barry, on Bee Gee wives, interview by Johnny Black, *Mojo*, June 2001.

George Harrison always said, 'You were four years later than us; we were four years earlier than you.' That's the way he put it to me, and I'd never known until then whether the Beatles even thought about the Bee Gees being around.

Barry, on George Harrison, interview by Timothy White, *Billboard*, March 24, 2001.

In 1978, the Bee Gees became one of the first group of musicians to be awarded a star on the Hollywood Walk of Fame. It can be seen at 6845 Hollywood Boulevard, Hollywood.

I said I wasn't sure how much longer I could keep doing this. And Paul [McCartney] said, 'Well, what else are you going to do?' And I just thought, 'Well, OK, then'.

Barry, on Paul McCartney and retirement, interview with Josh Eells, *Rolling Stone*, July 4, 2014.

All we heard around the house was 78's of the Glenn Miller Orchestra and the Mills Brothers. Dad loved their close harmony singing, and he taught us how to do it.

Maurice, on his dad's love of harmony, interview with Johnny Black, *Mojo*, May 21, 2001.

We were a family who had literally no money, and we could get $10 a show. We had to earn money; it couldn't be done any other way. We probably rented 20 houses during the seven years or so that we were in Australia. I think, without overemphasising it, my father just didn't pay the rent. We were that family in the middle of the night with the suitcases.

Barry, on family life in Australia, interview with Alexis Petridis, *Irish Times*, December 15, 2020.

> "
> We're persistent little buggers. We've had pitfalls, we've had valleys, we've had mountains. And if you didn't have the valleys you wouldn't know about the mountains.
> "

Maurice, about the group's endurance, In Conversation, May 21, 2001.

I like music that moves you emotionally, music where if you're in pain, it works for you. The first record I bought was 'Cryin' by Roy Orbison, and that destroyed me. I figured, 'There's a guy who's writing for people, who's writing for emotions.'

Barry, on music as emotion, *Australian Playboy*, 1990.

Who says you can't play different kinds of music? You just do what you want to do. We play different kinds of music because we put our hearts into different kinds of music.

Barry, on reinventing the band's sound, interview with Frank Rose, *Rolling Stone*, July 14, 1977.

66

There's fame and there's ultra-fame, and it can destroy you. You lose your perspective; you're in the eye of a hurricane, and you don't know you're there. And you don't know what tomorrow is; you don't know if what you're recording will be a hit or not. And we were kids, don't forget.

99

Barry, on fame, interview with Alexis Petridis, *Irish Times*, December 15, 2020.

The biggest hits written by
the Brothers Gibb, but recorded
by others:

"Come On Over"
Olivia Newton-John (1976)

"Love Me"
Yvonne Elliman (1976)

"More Than a Woman"
Tavares (1977)

"Grease" Frankie Valli (1978)

"Emotion"
Samantha Sang (1978)

"If I Can't Have You"
Yvonne Elliman (1978)

"Woman in Love"
Barbra Streisand (1980)

"Heartbreaker"
Dionne Warwick (1982)

"Islands in the Stream"
Dolly Parton and Kenny
Rogers (1983)

"Chain Reaction"
Diana Ross (1985)

Show business is something you have to have in you when you're born.
"

Robin, on the business of show, *Rolling Stone*, 1977.

Firstly, I think we give the public melodies. And secondly, we don't attempt to preach at people. There are so many groups which try to change the world. We, I think, are simply a pop group which writes all its own songs. We write songs about people and situations; we tell stories in our songs, but we don't give sermons.

Barry, on the band's philosophy, *Idea Special*, 1968.

153

We started singing on street corners and cinemas before the film started – it was kind of a grass roots kind of thing, very natural. My parents were a bit worried at first because they didn't know where it was going to end or whether they should encourage it.

Robin, on their early musical years, interview with Michael Odell, *Daily Express*, October 23, 1997

We don't sit down and say 'Alright, you think of the words and I'll think of the music.' There's no ego involved to the point where one would say, 'It's my idea, I'm going to finish the song.' There's none of that. If we get an idea, we bring it up and work on each other...bounce off each other.

"

Robin, on the song-writing process, interview by Paul Baratta, *Songwriter Magazine*, February 1978.

"
I do it when I love it
and I don't do it when
I don't feel like it.
"

Barry, on when he deploys his falsetto, interview by Johnny Black, *Mojo*, February 1998.

We trudged around Denmark Street, saw the manager of The Seekers, the manager of Cliff Richard, and they all told us we were wasting our time, groups were out. We were staying in a semi-detached in Hendon wondering what to do when my mother said we'd had a call from 'Robert Stickweed'. We had no idea who that was.

Maurice, on that fateful call from their future manager, Robert Stigwood, interview by Johnny Black, *Mojo*, June 2001.

Music is in the Bee Gees' blood. Their mother, Barbara, was a singer, and their father, Hugh, managed a dance band. Hugh was also the boys' manager, and encouraged them to sing in harmony.

I think Ed Sullivan had some kind of dementia, because he introduced us with the words, 'And now, a great group from England… Cary Grant.'

Robin, on their March 1968 *Ed Sullivan Show* debut, interview by Johnny Black, *Mojo*, June 2001.

66

We're just proud that we've been able to stay around as long as we have. When you consider that the average life span of a group is five years, no one is more amazed than we are.

99

Barry, on the band's enduring career, interview by Timothy White, *Billboard*, February 15, 1997.

Three brothers trying to be bigger than Beatles.

Maurice, on the group's lofty ambitions,
In Conversation, May 21, 2001.

The Bee Gees are
still – after forty years – the
proud creators of the
biggest-selling soundtrack
of all time (*Saturday
Night Fever*), with more than
45 million records sold.

It also won the 1978 Grammy
for Album of the Year.

It's hard to be an individual.
We don't really hang out
except when we're working.
But we work so much that
that's social for us, too.
So we don't need to go
to each other's houses.

Barry, on keeping a familial distance,
Denver Rocky Mountains News, 1997.

CHAPTER
SIX

COMEBACK KINGS

You can't keep a good Bee Gee down. From their early Beatles obsessions to their disco period, right through to their final reinvention as the masters of MOR, the Bee Gees proved that the key to longevity in the music business is stayin' alive without stayin' the same.

My tendency is not to listen to too much of our old stuff. I want to keep moving on and if I keep listening to things from the past, it might influence me in the wrong direction.

Barry, on moving forward, *Performing Songwriter*, 1998.

Most of the songs we've
written that have been
successful have been
written quickly – in
less than an hour.

Maurice, on the quick hits, *Still Waters Press Kit*, 1997.

A lot of bad records were made in that era, but the Bee Gees' songs hold up and will still be in clubs in 2050. It was exciting, progressive R&B, and the world went mad. The backlash was led by dinosaur critics who thought rock and heavy metal were the only music people should hear.

Robin, on the death of disco, *USA Today*, 1997.

We often wondered at what point in the industry does an artist become as important as an executive?

Barry, on the music industry, interview by Timothy White, *Billboard*, March 24, 2001.

As songwriters-for-hire, the Bee Gees have written more than one hundred Top Ten hits – including 17 No.1's – for other superstar artists spanning multiple genres, including Destiny's Child, Celine Dion, Elton John, Tom Jones, Dolly Parton, Diana Ross, Nina Simone, Rod Stewart, Barbra Streisand, Tina Turner, to name just a few.

They remain the only songwriters to ever have five songs simultaneously in the U.S. Top 10.

When I think about the *Fever* album, I don't think about disco. I only think about the recordings, and I have no negative feelings about them. These songs would have just been on our next album – not that soundtrack.

Barry, on *Saturday Night Fever*, interview by Timothy White, *Billboard*, March 24, 2001.

> **66**
> When we get together
> and write it's not like three
> individuals, it's like one
> person in the room.
> **99**

Maurice, on song-writing, interview with
Johnny Black, *Mojo*, May 21, 2001.

It's not explainable how it happened, but those songs seem to have penetrated the culture to the point that I don't think this music's going to be forgotten.

Barry, on the songs on *Saturday Night Fever*, interview with Alexis Petridis, *Irish Times*, December 15, 2020.

To have the music loved so much and then rejected out of hand within a decade... that creates hunger. You're determined to show it's not over.

Barry, on losing stardom after disco ran dry, *Entertainment Weekly*, 1997.

The first hit we had in Sydney, Australia, was 'Wine and Women'. But we had to buy out the record shops ourselves to give it a chance.

Robin, on their first hit, interview by Paul Baratta, *Songwriter Magazine*, February 1978.

We haven't peaked yet. The first and second times out the Bee Gees didn't quite make it all the way to the top. This time we have. And so far, there are no signs of levelling off.

Robin, on having a third try at fame, interview by Robert Windeler, *People Magazine*, June 2, 1978.

Even though we were
aged 8 to 11, the Gibb
name in Manchester was
like the Krays in London.

Barry, on life as a street kid, interview by
Michael Odell, *Daily Express*, October 23, 1997.

Maurice died when he was 53, in 2003. Robin died at the age of 62, in 2012.

Their younger brother, Andy Gibb, died at 30 in 1988. Barry is the only surviving brother of the Gibb family and has vowed to ensure the group's legacy outlives him.

We were proud fools,
too scared to admit
it at first, but we had
missed each other.

Robin, on their mid-1970s reconciliation, interview by
Michael Odell, *Daily Express*, October 23, 1997.

Three months before we moved back to England [in 1967], I was walking down the street in Sydney and I saw this Beatles fan club book, and I thought, 'Wow, look at the gear, look at the boots, look at the guitars.' Two months later, I was partying with them and hanging out with them in their inner circle. We had the same manager. It was totally unbelievable.

Maurice, on getting to know the Beatles, interview with Aidin Vaziri, *San Francisco Chronicle*, January 27, 2002.

We've never really enjoyed the idea of copying other people. We've come from the old school, where to have a style, to have a sound, and to be unique is more important than sounding like the No. 5 record on the chart.

Robin, on their unique sound, interviewed by Jane Stevenson, *Toronto Sun*, 2001.

"

We were living in Keppel Road, Chorlton-cum-Hardy, and the Gaumont cinema was our local. We used to go every Saturday for the Flash Gordon serials. This kid would get up in the interval and mime to Elvis records. We thought, 'God, we can do that.' The next week, we set off with a Tommy Steele record, 'Butterfingers', to mime to, but I dropped it and it broke.

"

Maurice, on the band's first gig, interview by Johnny Black, *Mojo*, June 2001.

People think it was the last thing he said – the remark about tossers – that made us walk off. It wasn't. It was the very first thing. We gave him a few more minutes out of professionalism…

Barry, about the now-infamous walk-out on Clive Anderson's talk show, interview by Johnny Black, *Mojo*, June 2001.

"

We'd been truanting, so we
pretended to be sick in bed.
I heard a policeman at the
door saying, 'Lads home, are
they?' and Dad said, 'Yes.'
He said, 'I've been having
a word with my sergeant.
They're thinking of emigrating
people to Australia. Have you
thought about that at all?'

"

Maurice, on emigrating to Australia, interview by
Johnny Black, *Mojo*, June 2001.

But the key to our success, I think, is the lyrics. People can listen to our lyrics and relate to what's happening. Everyone has loved somebody. Everybody knows what it's like staying alive.

Maurice, on the key to their success, *TG Magazine*, September 1978.

We want to do what we're doing right now until we drop. There's no age limit, you don't put an age limit on writing songs. Writing lasts forever. Beethoven wrote until he died. I mean no one came up to him and said, 'Hey, Ludwig, you're in your thirties!! You gotta quit!!'

Robin, on retirement, interview by Paul Baratta, *Songwriter Magazine*, February 1978.

Before the recording began, we were working in the middle of a speedway in Brisbane. In between each race, we would sing. This is a gig we conned our way into getting. They told us we could have whatever the crowd threw in the way of cash. So we would stand in the middle of the speedway and sing, and people would throw money onto the sawdust track, and we would run out on the track and pick it up. That was in 1959.

Barry, on their earliest performances, interview by Paul Baratta, *Songwriter Magazine*, February 1978.

"

Deep down we are
songwriters first and
foremost. We can write a
beautiful ballad and then
turn around and write...
a load of crap!

"

Maurice, on their song-writing peaks and troughs,
interview by Timothy White, *Rolling Stone*, May 17, 1979.

I hate disco music. I listen to it now and all I hear is a cymbal and a back-beat. The Bee Gees are a fly-by-night sort of group. We enjoy change and freshness, and disco was only one area we've delved into. I don't think we'll want to do it again.

Barry, on the noose known as disco, *Teen Beat*, 1980.

"

Oh, it's fucking deep – it's an endless, festering pit.

"

Maurice, when asked, "How deep is your love?", interview with David Wild, *Rolling Stone*, May 29, 1997.

We never completely
do a song just to please
ourselves. We bring
everybody we can into
the studio so that we can
get their opinions, even
the receptionist.

Barry, on focus-testing their songs, interview by
Timothy White, *Rolling Stone*, May 17, 1979.

People will be dancing to *Fever* in 2050. It's part of pop culture... just as much as the Beatles, Buddy Holly and Elvis Presley.

Robin Gibb, on *Saturday Night Fever, Denver Rocky Mountains News*, 1997.